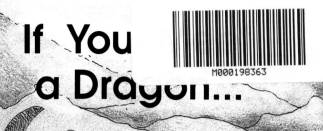

If You...
a Dragon...

Story by Joy Cowley
Illustrations by Rita Parkinson

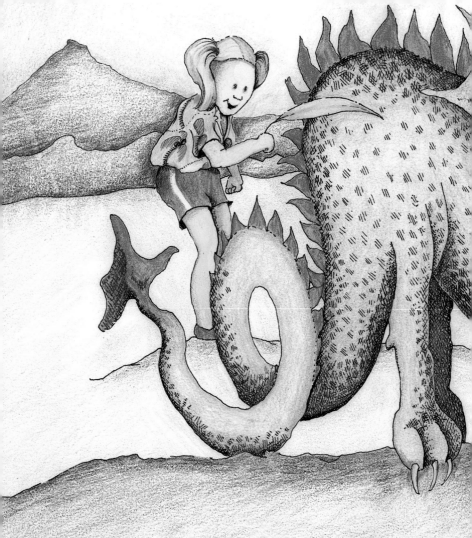

Tickle his back.

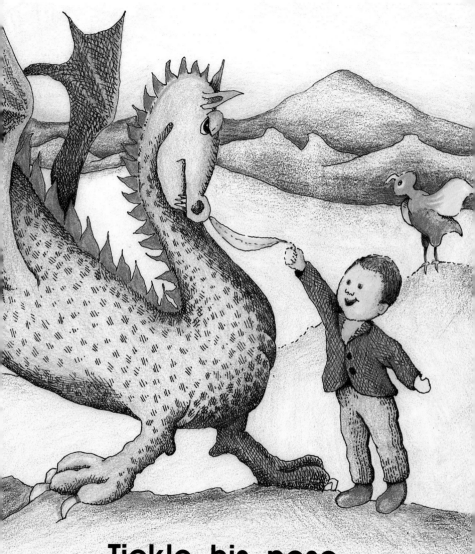

Tickle his nose.

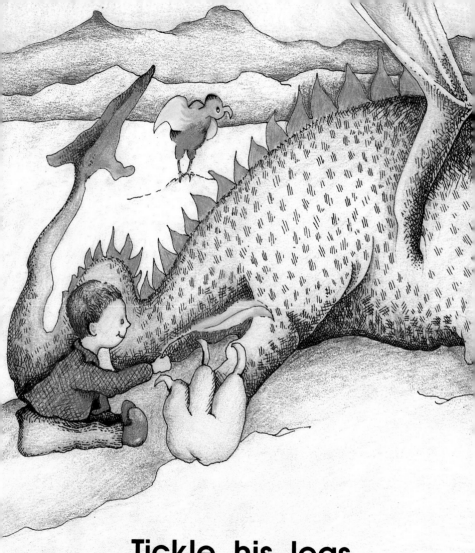

Tickle his legs.

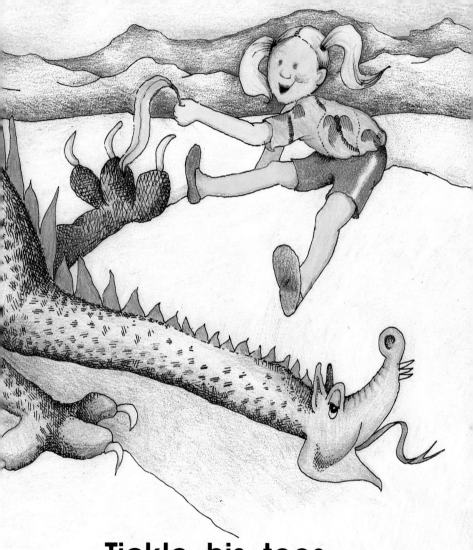

Tickle his toes.

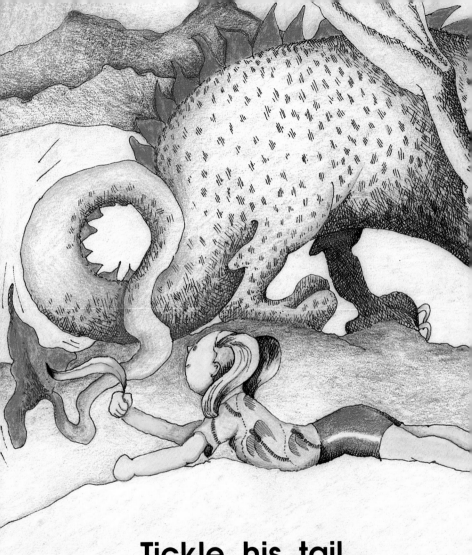

Tickle his tail.

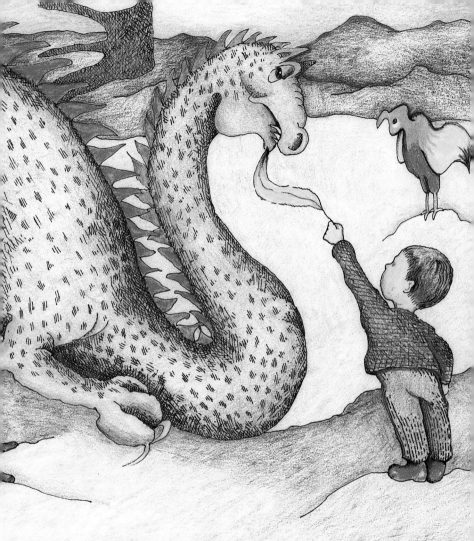

Tickle his chin...

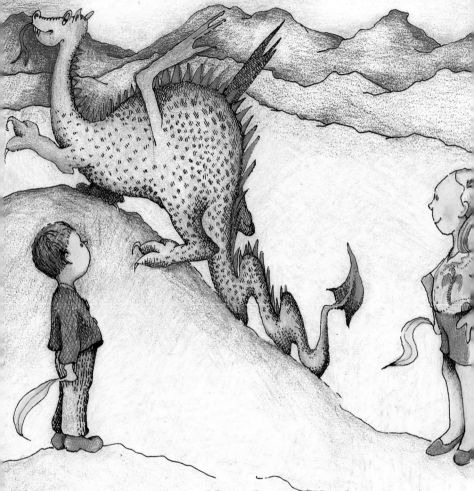

and that will be
the end of him.